Nelson

Literacy

Senior Authors
Miriam P. Trehearne
Jennette MacKenzie

Series Consultants and Writers
Maureen Dockendorf
Pat Horstead
Adrienne Gear
Heather McGowan—*Assessment*
Janice Novakowski—*Science*
Beth Zimmerman—*Word Work*
Marla Ciccotelli—*Word Work*
Maureen Innes—*ESL/ELL*
Nancy Christoffer—*Bias and Equity*

Susan Brown
Marg Camp
Kathleen Corrigan
Eileen Eby
Paula Goepfert
Jane Hutchison
Norma Kennedy
Bev McMorris

NELSON EDUCATION

NELSON EDUCATION

Nelson Literacy 2a

Miriam P. Trehearne
Jennette MacKenzie

Vice President, Publishing
Janice Schoening

General Manager, Literacy and Reference
Michelle Kelly

Publisher
Rivka Cranley

Managing Editor, Development
Lara Caplan

Senior Product Manager
Mark Cressman

Project Editor
Corry Codner

Developmental Editors
Tara Harte
David MacDonald
Caron Macmenamin

Researchers
Michelle Gram
Tara Harte
David MacDonald
Kim Toffan

Editorial Assistants
Kendel Doyle
Jenny Ellis
Hannah Gifford

Director, Content and Media Production
Carol Martin

Senior Content Production Editor
Susan Aihoshi

Copyeditor
Linda Jenkins

Proofreader
Sandra Manley

Production Manager
Helen Locsin

Production Coordinator
Vicki Black

Design Director
Ken Phipps

Series Design
Sasha Moroz

Series Wordmark
Steven Savicky

Cover Design
Sasha Moroz

Interior Design
Carianne Bauldry
Jarrel Breckon
Courtney Hellam
InContext Publishing
Jennifer Laing
Jennifer Leung
Sasha Moroz
Jan John Rivera

Asset Coordinators
Renée Ford
Suzanne Peden

Compositors
Carianne Bauldry
Courtney Hellam

Photo Research and Permissions
Julie Pratt

Cover Research
Natalie Russell

Printer
Transcontinental Printing

ISBN-13: 978-0-17-608934-4
ISBN-10: 0-17-608934-9

Printed and bound in Canada
2 3 4 5 12 11 10 09

For more information contact Nelson Education Ltd., 1120 Birchmount Road, Toronto, Ontario M1K 5G4. Or you can visit our Internet site at http://www.nelson.com.

Advisers and Reviewers

Gwen Babcock, Limestone DSB, ON

April Bell-Asselstine, Limestone DSB, ON

Ines Curiale, York CDSB, ON

Adrienne Gear, Vancouver SB, BC

Bernice Giancola, York Catholic DSB, ON

Joan Green, Calgary PSB, AB

Serena Hancock, NL

Lynne Healy, NS

Frances James, London DCSB, ON

Nicole Kelly, Nova Central School District, NL

Rebecca Kennedy, CDSB of Eastern Ontario, ON

Bonnie Lebowitz, Edmonton Public Schools, AB

Barb Mathiesson, North Vancouver SD, BC

Barb McBride, Vancouver SB, BC

Thérèse McNamara, Simcoe DSB, ON

Anthea Messersi, TDSB, ON

Alison Misa, York CDSB, ON

Linda Perrin, School District 8, NB

Katia Robles, TDSB, ON

Donna Robson, Cape Breton-Victoria Regional SB, NS

Joyce Rodway, NL

Nadia Russiello, York Region DSB, ON

Miranda Scenna, York Catholic DSB, ON

Susan Seeley, Toronto DSB, ON

Maryann Kennedy Smith, York Catholic DSB, ON

Yvette Sztorc, York Catholic DSB, ON

Mark Wilderman, Saskatoon PSD, SK

Contents

Social Studies

1 CELEBRATE TRADITIONS

Welcome to

Nelson Literacy

Your *Nelson Literacy* book is full of great stories and articles. Many of the topics are the same as those you will study in science and social studies.

Here are the different kinds of pages you will see in this book:

Let's Talk

Here's a chance to have some fun and show what you know.

Vocabulary

The vocabulary pages introduce you to words that you will find in the unit.

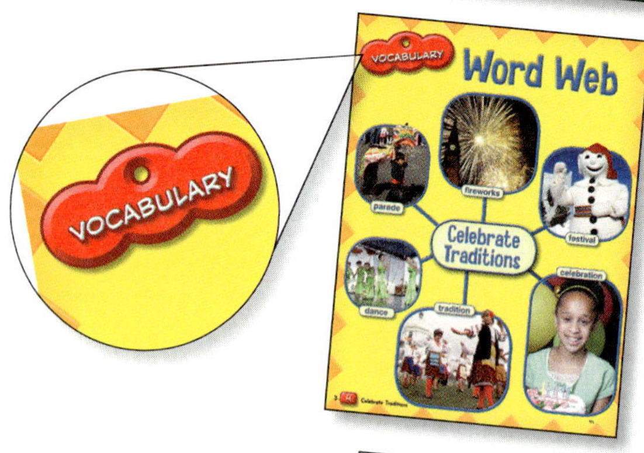

Let's Read, Let's Write, Let's Listen, Let's Speak, and Let's Look at Media

These pages tell you about reading, writing, listening, speaking, and media strategies. Some pages have sticky notes with hints about the strategies.

Try It Out

These pages give you the chance to try the strategies you've learned.

Literature

What Is a Story?

In this unit, you will

- make connections while you read
- identify characteristics of a story
- choose a big idea for writing
- look at book covers
- make connections while you listen

LET'S TALK

These pictures tell a story, but they are not in order. Change the order to show a story with a beginning, a middle, and an end. What title would you give the story?

VOCABULARY

WORDS FOR STORIES

Most stories have characters, settings, events, problems, and solutions. Look at these pictures from *Clara and the Bossy* to see this story's characteristics.

CHARACTERS
Clara, Madison, and their friends

SETTINGS
Madison's house and school

EVENT
Madison makes Clara feel bad about wearing her favourite dress.

PROBLEM
Madison makes fun of everybody.

SOLUTION
Clara decides to be herself.

THE TURNIP GARDEN

Written by Norma Kennedy
Illustrated by Helen Flook

> The beginning of a story tells you the characters and setting. Who is in this story? Where does it take place?

Papa and Mama and their three children lived in a teeny tiny house. The house had a teeny tiny garden. That was okay because they had only one turnip seed to plant.

Papa said he could dig the hole.

Mama said she could plant the seed.

Sister said she could water the garden.

Big Brother said he could pull the weeds.

What could Little Brother do to help?

The events of a story tell you what happens. What happens first in this story?

Papa dug the hole.

Mama planted the seed.

Sister watered the turnip garden.

Big Brother weeded the turnip garden.

Little Brother figured out how he could help. He sang to the turnip seed, “Grow, little turnip, grow.”

Every day, Sister watered the garden.

Every day, Big Brother pulled the weeds.

Every day, Little Brother sang, “Grow, little turnip, grow.”

The turnip started to grow bigger. It grew and grew and grew.

When the turnip grew bigger than the teeny tiny house, it was time to pull it up.

Papa pulled on the turnip. It didn't come up.

Mama pulled on Papa, who pulled on the turnip. It didn't come up.

Sister pulled on Mama, who pulled on Papa, who pulled on the turnip. It didn't come up.

Big Brother pulled on Sister, who pulled on Mama, who pulled on Papa, who pulled on the turnip.

The turnip still didn't come up.

> The middle of a story has a problem. What is the problem in the story?

They didn't know what to do. Little Brother said he knew what to do. He sang, "Come up, big turnip, come up."

Then Little Brother pulled on Big Brother, who pulled on Sister, who pulled on Mama, who pulled on Papa, who pulled on the gigantic turnip. And up it came!

The family ate delicious turnip every day for a very long time!

The ending of a story has a solution. How was the problem in this story solved?

PANCAKE SURPRISE

Written by Julie Stall
Illustrated by Jason Bone

Today was a special day for Leo. It was his mom's birthday. Leo wanted to make her the best breakfast ever! He decided to make her blueberry pancakes.

Leo mixed the pancake batter. He added the blueberries.

Leo's dad came into the kitchen. "What are you doing?" he said.

"I'm making Mom blueberry pancakes for her birthday breakfast."

His dad smiled.

Leo's dad poured the pancake batter into the pan. Leo used a spoon to try to make the pancakes look like hearts.

But the blueberries got crushed. "Oh, no!" said Leo. "These pancakes are a mess!"

Leo put syrup on the pancakes. They looked very bad. Leo tasted a pancake. It tasted good! That gave Leo an idea.

Leo brought the pancakes to his mom. He said, "Happy Birthday, Mom! Now open your mouth and close your eyes. You will get a big surprise!"

Leo's mom closed her eyes. Leo gave her a big bite. "This is good!" she said. "This is my best birthday ever!"

THINK ABOUT IT

What happens in the beginning, the middle, and the end of the story?

TRY IT OUT

Narrative

Hamster Chase

Based on the characters created by Ezra Jack Keats
Written by Anastasia Suen
Illustrated by Allan Eitzen

Peter took the hamster out of his cage.

"I'm going to miss you next week, Mikey," he said.

"Why?" asked Archie.

"It will be Amy's turn to take care of him," said Peter.

"Peter," said Amy, "I'm … ACHOO!"

Mikey jumped out of Peter's hand.

"Mikey!" said Peter. "Come back!"

"ACHOO!" said Amy.

"There goes Mikey!" said Archie. "He went into the coat closet."

"Come out, little guy," said Peter. "Hey! I have an idea."

"What?" asked Archie.

"We can make a trail of sunflower seeds back to Mikey's cage."

One, two, three ... Peter put the sunflower seeds in a line on the floor.

Mikey's nose popped out of the coat closet.

"It's working!" said Amy.

“How will we get him back into the cage?” asked Archie.

“We can make stairs with these books,” said Peter.

“Put a few sunflower seeds on the books, too,” said Amy.

Nibble-nibble, nibble-nibble.

Mikey ate his way out of the closet.

“It’s working,” said Archie.

Nibble-nibble, nibble-nibble.

Mikey ate his way up to the first book.

“Go up the stairs, little guy,” said Peter.

Nibble-nibble, nibble-nibble.

"ACHOO!" said Amy.

Mikey jumped into his cage.

"You did it!" said Archie.

"Mikey's fur makes me sneeze," said Amy. "Peter, will you take care of Mikey for me next week?"

"You have a deal," said Peter.

THINK ABOUT IT

What was the problem in the story? How was the problem solved?

TRY IT OUT

Narrative

THE WILD, WOOLLY CHILD

Written by Joy Cowley
Illustrated by Philip Webb

The wild, woolly child was very wild and very woolly.

The wild, woolly child chased lions up ladders.

She chased baggy elephants over rooftops.

"Our child is too wild and too woolly," said Mother.

"Yes," said Father. "Our child is too woolly and too wild."

"Listen to us!" the hair people called. "Your child is wild because she's woolly. We'll give her a haircut and take all the wildness out of her."

Number One took out her scissors. Snip, snip, woollygrunch! The scissors broke in two!

Number Two took out his clippers.
Clip, clip, woollygrunch!
The clippers broke in two!

Number Three took out her chainsaw.
Brrrm, brrrm, went the chainsaw.
Brrrm, brrrm—WOOLLYGRUNCH!
The chainsaw broke into little bits.
The wild and woolly child laughed and laughed and laughed.

Mother and Father took the wild, woolly child home.

"You know something?" said Mother. "I like our child wild and woolly."

"You know something?" said Father. "So do I."

So the wild, woolly child stayed wild and woolly.

She chased lions up ladders.

She chased baggy elephants over rooftops.

And sometimes … she chased the hair people down the street.

THINK ABOUT IT

What was the problem in the story? How was the problem fixed?

Let's Listen

The Bear

Traditional Song
Illustrated by Mike Dietz

Listen for things that connect to your own life.

The other day
I met a bear
Up in the woods
A way up there

He looked at me
I looked at him
He sized up me
I sized up him

And so I ran
Away from there
And right behind
Me was that bear

Ahead of me
I saw a tree
A great big tree
Oh, golly gee

The lowest branch
Was ten feet up
I had to jump
And trust my luck

And so I jumped
Into the air
But I missed that branch
On the way up there

Now don't you fret
And don't you frown
I caught that branch
On the way back down

That's all there is
There is no more
Until I meet
That bear once more

Listen for things that connect to other songs you know.

Choose a Big Idea

What holds all your school supplies together? Your backpack.

Your writing is like your backpack. One big idea holds all the little ideas together. The big idea is called the main idea.

Today we went on a school trip to the farm. We passed a field with cows. My favourite drink is juice. I fell asleep on the bus. The farm had lots of animals.

Last week my dog ran away from home. I looked for him in the park across the street. I looked for him in the schoolyard around the corner. I finally found him playing in my own backyard. He came home all by himself.

LET'S LOOK AT MEDIA

Identify Purpose and Audience

Tell a Book by Its Cover

A book cover gives readers hints about what is inside the book. The picture on the cover helps readers decide if they want to read the book.

The title gives you an idea of what the book is about. What do you think this book will be about?

The cover picture is used to catch your attention. What is there about this picture that catches your attention?

Look at this book cover. What do you think this book will be about? Does the picture make you want to read the book? Why?

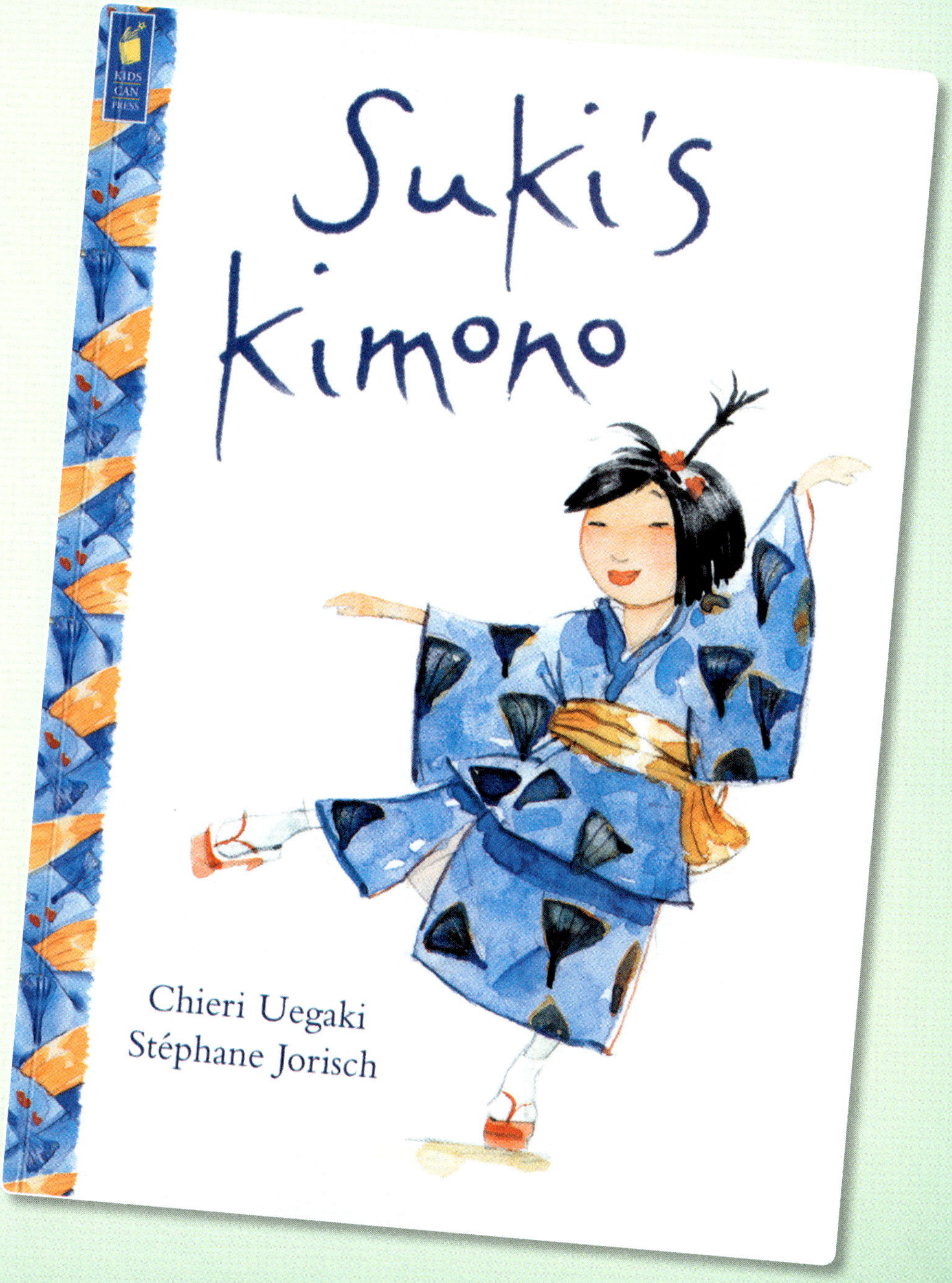

IT'S NOT MY FAULT!

Written and illustrated by Nancy Carlson

Think about what you already know. Why does your principal call students to the office?

On Monday afternoon, George was called to Principal Flom's office.

"Come in, George," began Ms. Flom. "I'd like to … "

But before she could finish, George blurted out, "I can explain everything! I was late today, but **it's not my fault!**"

"This morning I overslept. I had to run in the halls to get to class on time. A kindergartner bumped into me, and I was late to class.

"So, it's all the kindergartner's fault I was late today."

"Well, George … ," said Ms. Flom.

"All right! I didn't catch these mice, but **it's not my fault!**

"I was carrying the blue paint to my desk. **It's not my fault** I tripped!"

Think about what is happening in the story. How did you feel when you were late?

Connect to events in real life. What does it mean to be on the school patrol?

"While I was cleaning it up, that cage just fell over.

"I was trying to catch the mice when I was called to your office. So, **it's all *your* fault** I didn't catch … ?"

"George!" exclaimed Ms. Flom. "I wanted to ask you to be on the school patrol. But it's not *my* fault we can't discuss that today! You'll be busy cleaning up that paint, and … CATCHING THESE MICE!"

When George finally got home, his mother said, "YOU'RE LATE!"

"I can explain," mumbled George. "Ms. Flom made me stay after school to clean up paint and catch mice, and it's all my fault."

"Why is that?" asked his mother.

"Because I have a big mouth!"

Connect to another story you have read like this one. How was it the same?

Jon looked into Snowball's eyes.

He didn't blink.

And he didn't blink.

And he still didn't blink.

Snowball just stared.

Jon's eyes began to hurt … and shake … and … blink!

"I don't believe it," Jon said. "Snowball is the Blink-master!"

"Cats hardly ever blink, didn't you know?" Sally smiled.

THINK ABOUT IT

Think about a time when you were in a contest. How does making this connection help you know how Jon and Sally felt?

OONGA BOONGA

Excerpted from *Oonga Boonga* by Frieda Wishinsky
Illustrated by Carol Thompson

Nobody could make Baby Louise stop crying.

Her mother tried. She held her close and sang a little lullaby.

But that didn't help.

Her father tried. He rocked her gently in his arms and whispered softly in her ear.

But that didn't help.

Then her brother, Daniel, came home from school.

"Oonga boonga," he said to Louise.

Louise looked up, tears streaming down her face.

"Oonga boonga," he repeated.

Louise stopped sobbing and looked him straight in the eye.

"Oonga boonga," said Daniel again.

Louise broke into a smile.

“How did you do that?” asked his mother.

“It’s easy. You just say ‘oonga boonga,’” said Daniel.

“Oonga boonga,” said his mother.

“Oonga boonga,” said his father.

“See,” said Daniel. “She likes it.”

And sure enough, she did.

Louise was smiling from ear to ear.

“I’m going out to play,” said Daniel.

But as soon as he left, Louise's smile faded.

Soon she was crying as loudly as before.

"Oonga boonga," said her mother.

"Oonga boonga," said her father.

But nothing helped. Louise kept on crying.

"What's wrong?" said Daniel.

"Oonga boonga doesn't work anymore," they said.

Daniel leaned over Louise and whispered in her ear, "Bonka wonka, Louise."

And Louise stopped crying.

THINK ABOUT IT

What connections did you make in this story?

TRY IT OUT

Make Connections

I Wanna Iguana

Written by Karen Kaufman Orloff
Illustrated by David Catrow

Dear Mom,

I know you don't think I should have Mikey Gulligan's baby iguana when he moves, but here's why I should. If I don't take it, he goes to Stinky and Stinky's dog, Lurch, will eat him. You don't want that to happen, do you?

Signed,
Your sensitive son,
Alex

Dear Alex,

I'm glad you're so compassionate, but I doubt that Stinky's mother will let Lurch get into the iguana's cage.

Nice try, though.

Love,
Mom

Dear Mom,

You would never even have to see the iguana. I'll keep his cage in my room on the dresser next to my soccer trophies. Plus, he's so small, I bet you'll never even know he's there.

Love and a zillion and one kisses,

Alex

Dear Alex,

Iguanas can grow to be over two metres long. You won't have enough space in your whole room, much less on your dresser (with or without your trophies).

Love,

Mom

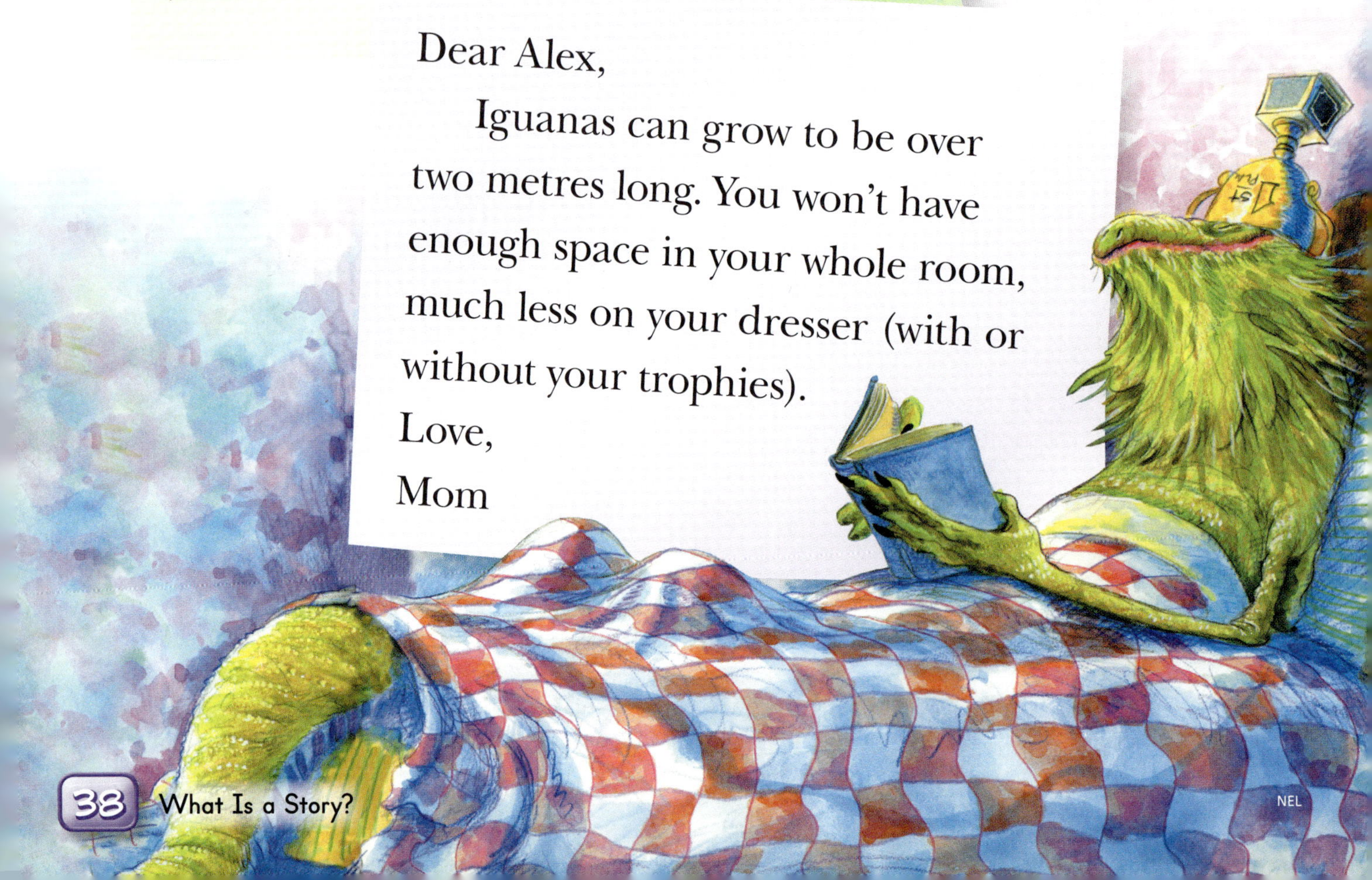

Dear Mom,

This iguana can be the brother I've always wanted.

Love,

Your lonely child, Alex

Dear Alex,

You have a brother …

Okay, Let's say I let you have the iguana on a trial basis. What exactly would you do to take care of it?

Love,

Mom

Dear Mom,

I would feed him every day (he eats lettuce), make sure he had enough water, and I would clean his cage when it got messy.

Love,

Responsible Alex

P.S. What's a trial basis?

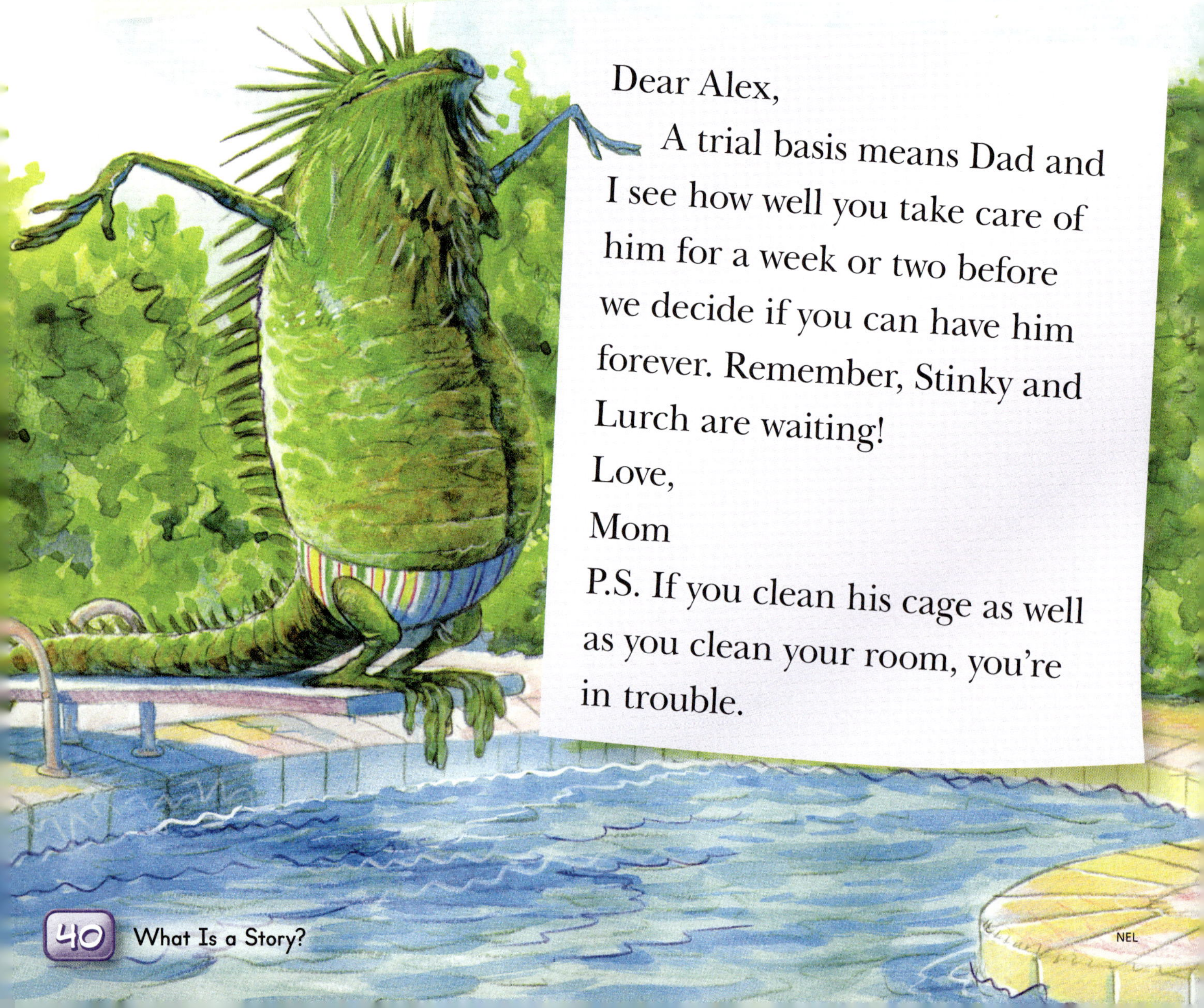

Dear Alex,

A trial basis means Dad and I see how well you take care of him for a week or two before we decide if you can have him forever. Remember, Stinky and Lurch are waiting!

Love,

Mom

P.S. If you clean his cage as well as you clean your room, you're in trouble.

"Are you sure you want to do this Alex?"

"Yes, Mom!
I wanna iguana …
Please!"

Dear Alex,
Look on your dresser.
Love,
Mom

"Yessss! Thank you! Thank you!"

THINK ABOUT IT

Think about a time you really wanted something. How did making this connection help you know how Alex felt?

ANIMALS

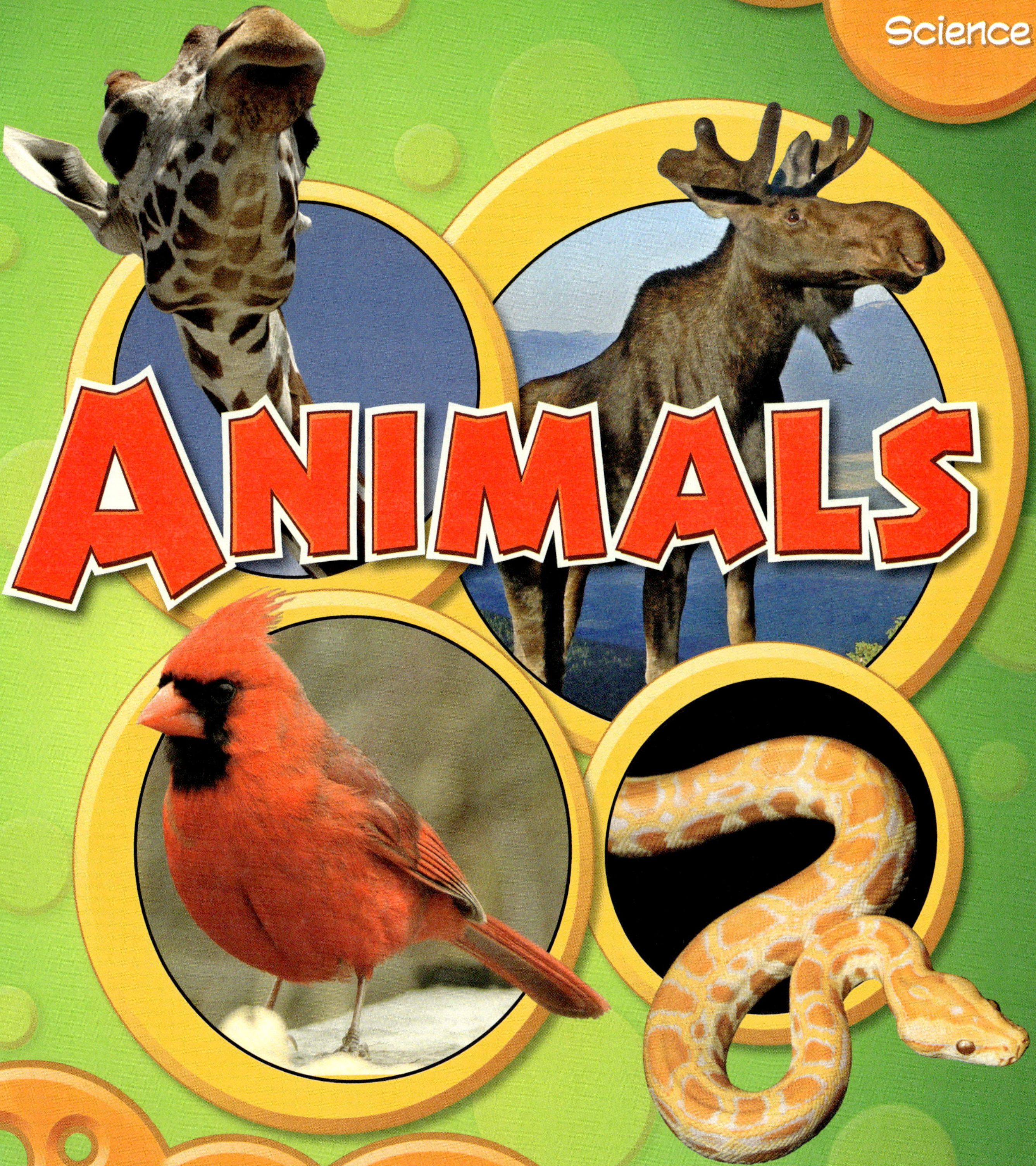

In this unit, you will

- visualize while you read
- visualize while you listen
- read information reports
- add details to your writing
- look at trading cards
- learn about animals

LET'S TALK

BABIES

Match each baby animal with an adult animal.

Tell two things you know about each animal.

ADULTS

VOCABULARY

Words About Animals

Size

How Animals Move

Animal Bodies

What other words about animals do you know?

HOW BIG?

by Katharine Kenah

Look for words that help you make a picture in your mind. What words help you visualize?

Animals are all around you.

Some animals are too small to see.
A flea is very tiny.

Some animals are big beasts.
An elephant is enormous!

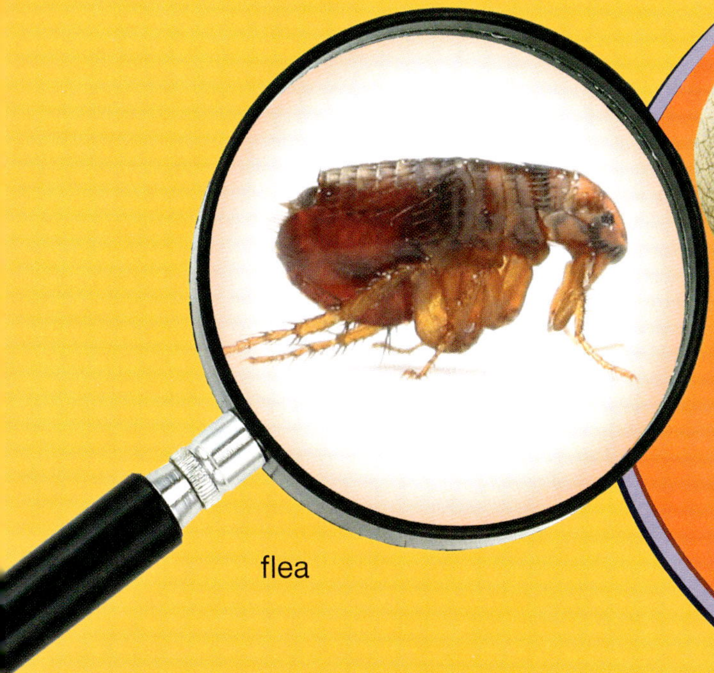
flea

elephant

KOMODO DRAGON

The komodo dragon is the biggest lizard in the world.

It is longer than a picnic table.

GIRAFFE

The giraffe is the tallest animal in the world.

It is about as tall as a two-storey house.

Think about what you already know. Would a giraffe be as tall as your home?

SIBERIAN TIGER

The Siberian tiger is the biggest cat in the world.

It is as long as two bathtubs.

STICK INSECT

The stick insect is the longest insect in the world.

It is about as long as a ruler.

Think about what you already know. Can you visualize how long your ruler is?

GOLIATH BEETLE

The goliath beetle is one of the biggest bugs in the world.

It is about as big as your hand.

BLUE WHALE

The blue whale is the biggest animal in the world.

It is as long as three school buses.

TRY IT OUT

Visualize

Odd Birds

by Teresa Domnauer

Some birds are noisy. Some birds are tiny.

Some birds are colourful. And some birds are just odd!

parrots

Ostrich

This odd bird is an ostrich.

It grows taller than most people.

ostrich

hummingbird

Hummingbird

This odd bird is a hummingbird.

It lays eggs the size of jellybeans.

Pelican

This odd bird is a pelican.

It uses its pouch like a net to scoop up fish.

pelican

THINK ABOUT IT

Find a place in the text where visualizing helped you understand what you were reading.

TRY IT OUT

Visualize

JUMP OR JIGGLE

by Evelyn Beyer

caterpillar

horses

Frogs jump
Caterpillars hump

Worms wiggle
Bugs jiggle

Rabbits hop
Horses clop

Snakes slide
Seagulls glide

Mice creep
Deer leap

Puppies bounce
Kittens pounce

Lions stalk—
But—
I walk!

seagull

lion

THINK ABOUT IT

How did making pictures in your mind help you understand what you were reading?

TRY IT OUT

Visualize

HOW POLAR BEARS HUNT

by Chelsea Donaldson

A giant polar bear sits very still beside an ice hole. It sits so still, it looks like a lump of ice. A big seal pokes its head out of the water.

A polar bear sits on the ice.

A polar bear has big claws.

Quickly, the bear uses its strong mouth and sharp claws to pull the seal out of the water.

The seal wiggles and struggles to get free. Then it stops moving.

Seals live in water and on land.

The bear carries the dead seal to its den.

It is a mother bear, and she shares the seal with her two hungry cubs.

The seal is enough food to last the bears for a few days.

Polar bear cubs wait in their den.

Seal is the polar bear's favourite food. Bears also hunt animals such as walrus, reindeer, seabirds, and fish. They sometimes even hunt and kill beluga whales.

It takes a big meal to fill up a polar bear!

Polar bears hunt beluga whales.

THINK ABOUT IT

How did visualizing help you understand what you were reading?

All About Frogs

by Michael Musiba

The title tells you what the report is about. What is this information report about?

Frog Bodies

Frogs use their strong back legs to jump. They can travel far in just one jump.

Many frogs are great swimmers. Their webbed feet help them swim fast. Webbed feet have skin between the toes.

Did you know that not all frogs are green? Some frogs are red or blue or yellow. Some even have stripes or spots.

Life Cycle of a Frog

Here is what happens in the life cycle of a frog.

1. A mother frog lays many eggs like this one.

2. A tadpole grows inside each egg. Then it breaks out and swims away.

3. The tadpole grows four legs. Its tail gets shorter and shorter.

4. Now it is a frog.

Many frogs live in water and on land.

Frog Homes

Lots of frogs live near water. You'll see them around ponds and lakes.

Have you ever seen a frog in a tree? Some frogs spend their whole lives in trees. They never come down!

Tree frogs have sticky suckers on their toes. The suckers help them stick to leaves so they don't fall.

Each section tells you information. What do you learn about frogs in this section?

The gold frog is tiny.

The goliath frog is huge.

Big and Small Frogs

Different kinds of frogs are different sizes. The gold frog is one of the smallest frogs in the world.

The biggest frog in the world is the same size as a pet cat! It is called a goliath frog.

Each section tells you information. What do you learn about frogs in this section?

TRY IT OUT

Information Report

OWLS

by Adrienne Mason

KINDS OF OWLS

There are different kinds of owls.

Many owls have flat, wide faces.

great grey owl

snowy owl

barn owl

OWL BODIES

Each part of an owl's body has a job to do.

Wings

Owls use their wings to fly.

Ears

Owls use their ears to listen for animals to hunt.

THINK ABOUT IT

What information about owls did you learn from this report?

TRY IT OUT

Information Report

A Long Winter Sleep

by Elizabeth MacLeod

Be quiet when you walk through a forest in winter. Animals may be sleeping!

Some animals sleep all winter long. This sleep is called hibernation.

Why Animals Hibernate

There is not much food around in winter. Animals do not eat when they hibernate. Hibernation helps animals live through the winter.

The jumping mouse hibernates.

Getting Ready to Hibernate

When fall comes, animals that hibernate begin to eat a lot. They need to get fat before their long winter sleep.

The animals look for a safe place to hibernate.

Groundhogs get fat before they hibernate.

A groundhog hibernates in a hole.

Animals That Hibernate

Here are some animals that hibernate.

Groundhogs are also called woodchucks. They take only one breath every three or four minutes when they hibernate.

Lots of garter snakes come together to hibernate. They hibernate in tree stumps, in piles of rocks, or underground.

Garter snakes come out of hibernation in the spring.

Little brown bats hibernate.

Little brown bats like to hibernate in caves. They hang upside down in large groups.

Do bears hibernate? They sleep most of the winter, but they are not really hibernating. They sometimes wake up and go for a walk.

Bears do not hibernate.

THINK ABOUT IT

What information about hibernating animals did you learn from this report?

TRY IT OUT

Information Report

ANIMAL GROUPS

by Etta Kaner

People like to group together things that are the same in some ways. Scientists group together animals. Some of these groups you already know, like fish and birds.

What are some other animal groups? What is the same about the animals in each group? Read on to find the answers.

How are all fish the same?

Great white sharks are fish.

FISH

Fish are animals that live only in water. They can be tiny or as large as sharks. No matter what size, all fish have fins to help them swim.

All fish breathe through gills. Gills are the flaps you see on each side of a fish's body.

MAMMALS

All baby mammals drink milk from their mothers. This is true for young bats and lions. That is why these two very different animals belong in the same group.

All mammals have fur or hair on their skin.

Raccoons are mammals.

Short-horned lizards are reptiles.

REPTILES

Animals with dry, scaly skin are reptiles. The scales are made of keratin. That's what your fingernails are made of! The scales may be smooth, like they are on a snake, or rough, like they are on a lizard.

Penguins are birds.

BIRDS

An animal is a bird if it has feathers. Feathers keep birds warm. They also help most birds, like robins, fly. Some birds, like penguins, don't fly at all.

AMPHIBIANS

An amphibian spends part of its time on land and part of its time in water. Can you think of any animals like this? Frogs and toads, of course!

Salamanders are amphibians. They may look like lizards, but they're not.

Blue-spotted salamanders are amphibians.

INSECTS

Are ants, butterflies, and bees insects? Yes, they are. Like all insects, they have six legs. Insects also have a hard skin on their bodies.

Bees are insects.

THINK ABOUT IT

What information about animal groups did you learn from this report?

Mice

Written by Rose Fyleman
Illustrated by Sally Wern Comport

I think mice
Are rather nice.

Their tails are long,
Their faces small,
They haven't any
Chins at all.

Listen for words that help you make pictures in your mind.

Their ears are pink,
Their teeth are white,
They run about
The house at night.
They nibble things
They shouldn't touch
And no one seems
To like them much.

Listen for words you can connect to.

But *I* think mice
Are nice.

Animal Trading Cards

There are all kinds of trading cards.
Some are about animals.

The front of the trading card tells you what it is about.

The back gives you facts. What facts do you learn about the beaver?

What do you learn from each side of this trading card?

Add Details to Your Writing

Details help the reader visualize what you are writing about.

My Pet by Deena

I have a pet. His name is Walter. We have lots of fun together.

My Pet by Deena

I have a pet cat. His name is Walter. We have fun playing together. I throw his toy mouse and he chases after it.

ANIMALS IN INUIT LIFE

by Walter Zim

Animals were important in Inuit life long ago. There were no stores for Inuit people to buy what they needed. They got nearly everything they needed from animals.

Homes

In spring and summer, Inuit families lived in tents. The tents were made with skin from caribou and seals.

Inuit lived in tents in the summer.

Inuit hunted caribou.

Clothes

Inuit used skin and fur from animals to make clothes. They used caribou skin and seal fur to make warm clothes for winter.

Food

Inuit got nearly all their food from animals. They hunted whales, seals, and caribou. Sometimes they also hunted smaller animals, like the Arctic hare and the Arctic fox.

This fur coat is called a parka.

The fur of the Arctic fox was also used to make clothes.

The Arctic hare can dig in the snow to hide from hunters.

Respect for Animals

Inuit were thankful that animals gave them many things they needed. They used nearly every part of an animal for something. Inuit never hunted animals just for fun.

Inuit Today

Today, Inuit live in modern homes and shop in stores. Some Inuit still hunt animals, just like Inuit of long ago.

Inuit made doll clothes from leftover fur.

This sleeping bag is made from caribou skin.

THINK ABOUT IT

What details did the author write that helped you visualize?

Social Studies

Celebrate Traditions

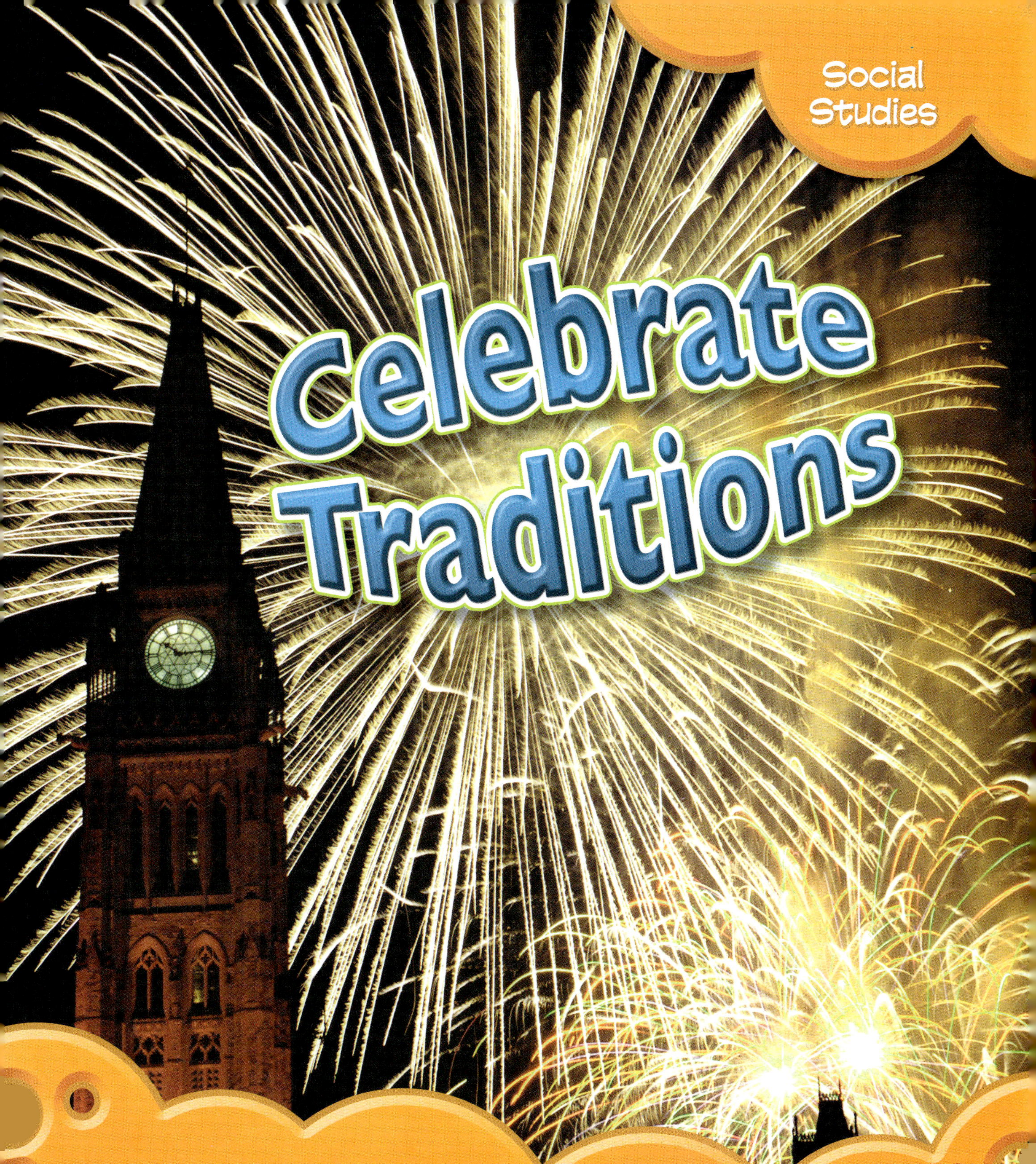

In this unit, you will

- predict while you read
- stay on topic while you write
- read titles and headings
- listen for descriptive words
- learn about traditions and celebrations
- look at invitations

LET'S TALK

Remembrance Day

Hanukkah

Powwow

Look at the pictures. What do you know about these celebrations and traditions?

Caribana

Chinese New Year

Christmas

VOCABULARY

Word Web

Celebrate Traditions

fireworks

parade

festival

dance

tradition

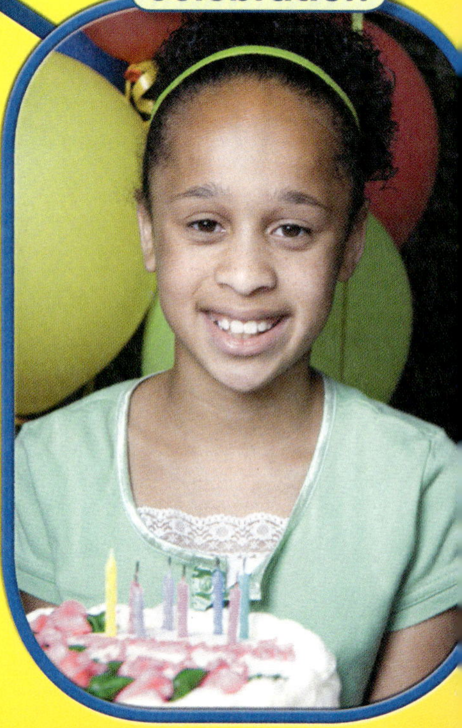

celebration

Hooray for Canada Day!

by Valerie Wyatt

A title tells you what the text is about. What do you think this text will be about?

July 1 is Canada Day. How do you celebrate? Some people have a party. Others dress in red and white to match Canada's flag. Fireworks are often part of the fun. There are many ways to celebrate Canada Day!

Headings tell you what each section of the text is about. What is this section of the text about?

Taste the Cake

There are clowns and a huge Canada Day cake at Vancouver's Capilano Suspension Bridge. Bring your appetite and join the fun.

Feel the Dance

If you like to dance, celebrate Canada Day in Red Deer. And don't miss the storytelling and fireworks.

See the Planes

In Canada's capital, Ottawa, the Snowbirds put on an air show. There are also fireworks and a ceremony for new Canadians.

Headings tell you what each section of the text is about. What do you think you'll learn in this section?

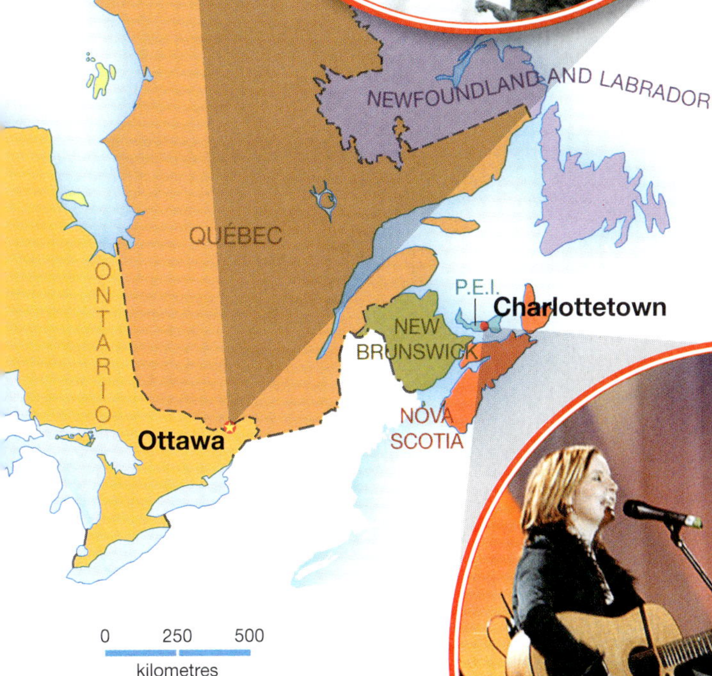

Hear the Music

A 10-hour concert is part of Canada Day in Charlottetown. After dark, the sky lights up with fireworks.

My Turn to Remember

Written by Tara Harte
Illustrated by Claire Fletcher

A Special Day

Today is November 11.

Remembrance Day.

We are having an assembly in the gym.

My class is the first to go on stage.

An Important Poem

I'm nervous.

We are saying a poem.

A soldier named John McCrae wrote it.

I'm the first person to say my lines.

What if I make a mistake?

Finding My Courage

My teacher nods at me to start.
I look at all the students in the gym.
I look up at the Canadian flag.
I think of the brave soldiers who fought
to keep Canada safe.

Saying My Lines

I touch the red poppy on my shirt.

I swallow, and then say,

"In Flanders Fields the poppies blow

Between the crosses, row on row …"

THINK ABOUT IT

How did the title and headings help you predict what the text was about?

TRY IT OUT

Titles and Headings

NOISY CELEBRATIONS

by Elizabeth MacLeod

People all over Canada like to get together to celebrate. It is fun to make noise at celebrations!

JINGLE DANCES

Some First Nations girls and women do jingle dances at powwows. They wear special clothes called jingle dresses. Their dresses have many rows of metal cones. The cones jingle when they hit each other.

The cones on this girl's dress make a jingling sound when she dances.

HAPPY NEW YEAR!

Long ago, people made noise on New Year's Eve to scare away bad spirits. Today, we still blow horns and kazoos. We also yell, "Happy New Year!"

Everyone yells, "Happy New Year!" at midnight.

Horns and noisemakers can make a lot of noise!

UGLY STICKS

In Newfoundland, people make noise with ugly sticks. Ugly sticks are mop handles with bells, horns, and bottle caps nailed to them.

People at parties tap the ugly stick on the floor. They also hit it with a drumstick or a piece of wood to make more noise.

Ugly sticks have colourful faces.

Some ugly sticks have a boot or rubber on the bottom.

THINK ABOUT IT

Which headings helped you the most to know what the section was about?

TRY IT OUT

Titles and Headings

WHAT'S FOR DINNER?

by Norma Kennedy

My family loves food from different countries. In Canada, there is so much to choose from. Today I asked, "What's for dinner?" Everyone had a different answer.

Let's Go Italian!

My brother wanted to go to a restaurant for spaghetti. The owners came to Canada from Italy. They make their own spaghetti and other pastas. They also make really good tomato sauce. They told us that the Italian word *spaghetti* means "little strings."

Buy Thai!

Dad said he'd go to the store to get what he needed to make a Thai dinner. Thai food comes from Thailand, a country in Asia. Thai food is popular all over the world.

What will Dad buy for a Thai dinner? Rice, fresh herbs, and fish sauce are all used in Thai food. My favourite is green chicken curry. It isn't really made with green chicken! Chili peppers and fresh herbs make the curry sauce green.

Bring Samosas Home!

Mom wanted to order in her favourite Indian dishes. Samosas are pastry triangles filled with spiced vegetables or meat. Butter chicken has a smooth, buttery sauce. Naan is a round flatbread that goes with everything.

How did we decide what to have for dinner? Well, we have a special tool that helps us make important decisions.... It is the spinner you see below!

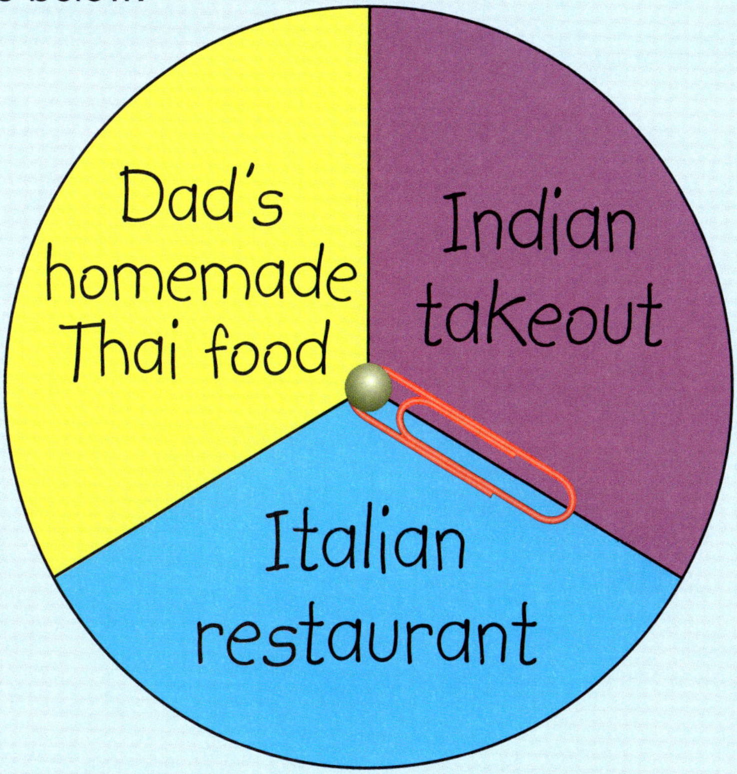

THINK ABOUT IT

Which heading helped you predict? Which heading didn't? What heading would you use instead?

A Thanksgiving Dinner

by Maude M. Grant

Listen for words that help you create a picture in your mind.

Take a turkey, stuff it fat,
Some of this and some of that.
Get some turnips, peel them well.
Cook a big squash in its shell.

Now potatoes, big and white,
Mash till they are soft and light.
Cranberries, so tart and sweet,
With the turkey we must eat.

Pickles—yes—and then, oh my!
For a dessert a pumpkin pie,
Golden brown and spicy sweet.
What a fine Thanksgiving treat!

A New Year for Everyone

by Evan Park

The title helps you predict what the text will be about. What do you think this text will be about?

Many Canadians celebrate the New Year at midnight on December 31. They sing, blow kazoos, and cheer. But some Canadian families celebrate the New Year on different days and in different ways.

Chinese New Year

Chinese New Year is celebrated in January or February. It lasts for fifteen days. Chinese Canadians clean their homes to sweep away bad luck and make room for good luck. They also hang red decorations and put out fruit. Adults give children red envelopes with money inside!

Red is the colour for good luck and happiness.

The Midwinter Festival ends with a dance to thank the Three Sisters—corn, beans, and squash.

A Midwinter Festival

Iroquois people celebrate the New Year in January or February. They dress in traditional clothing and perform songs and dances. There are chanting ceremonies, too. People also share dreams they have had. The festival lasts for eight days.

Headings help you predict what each section will be about. What do you think this section will be about?

These little lamps are called diyas.

Headings help you predict what each section will be about. What do you think this section will be about?

Stop and check your prediction. Were you right?

Diwali

Hindu people celebrate Diwali, the festival of lights. Diwali is in October or November. Little oil lamps or candles are lit to honour the goddess of good fortune, wealth, and happiness. People exchange gifts, such as candy and clothes. They eat special foods with friends and family.

A shofar is a trumpet made from a ram's horn.

Rosh Hashanah

Rosh Hashanah is the Jewish New Year. It is celebrated in early autumn. During Rosh Hashanah, people think about mistakes they made in the past and look forward to a new year. People eat holiday food such as honey cake. At prayer services, a shofar is blown.

Apples dipped in honey are a traditional Rosh Hashanah treat.

KWANZAA FUN

by Jeffrey Williams

Kwanzaa is a time for us to remember our African heritage. Kwanzaa lasts from December 26 through January 1. We light a special candle each day.

We light seven candles during Kwanzaa— one for each day of celebration.

Yummy Treats

We eat special foods during Kwanzaa. We might have peanut soup or coconut sweets. Sometimes, we have fried bananas or sweet potato pie.

We eat meals with our families during Kwanzaa.

Colourful Decorations

We decorate our homes in red, green, and black. They are the colours of Kwanzaa. We hang special art and African cloth on the walls. It is fun to make decorations, too.

Fun with Friends

We see friends. We sing, dance, and play drums. We buy or make gifts for our friends and families. Our parents show us how to make drums, rattles, and rain sticks.

We have fun playing Kwanzaa drums.

THINK ABOUT IT

How did the headings help you predict what each section of the text was about?

TRY IT OUT

Predict

FOUR SEASONS OF CELEBRATING

by Greg Kucharic

Canadians like to celebrate all year long—winter, spring, summer, and autumn.

WINTER CARNIVAL FUN

Québec City has a Winter Carnival every February. Carnival's symbol is a huge white snowman called Bonhomme. If you go to the Winter Carnival, watch for people racing canoes across the St. Lawrence River. Maybe you'd like to try ice wall climbing!

MAPLE SYRUP IN SPRING

Maple syrup festivals happen all across Canada in March and April. People eat maple treats, such as maple taffy and pancakes covered in maple syrup. They also go on horse-drawn sleigh rides. They visit old-fashioned sugar shacks and compete in log-sawing competitions.

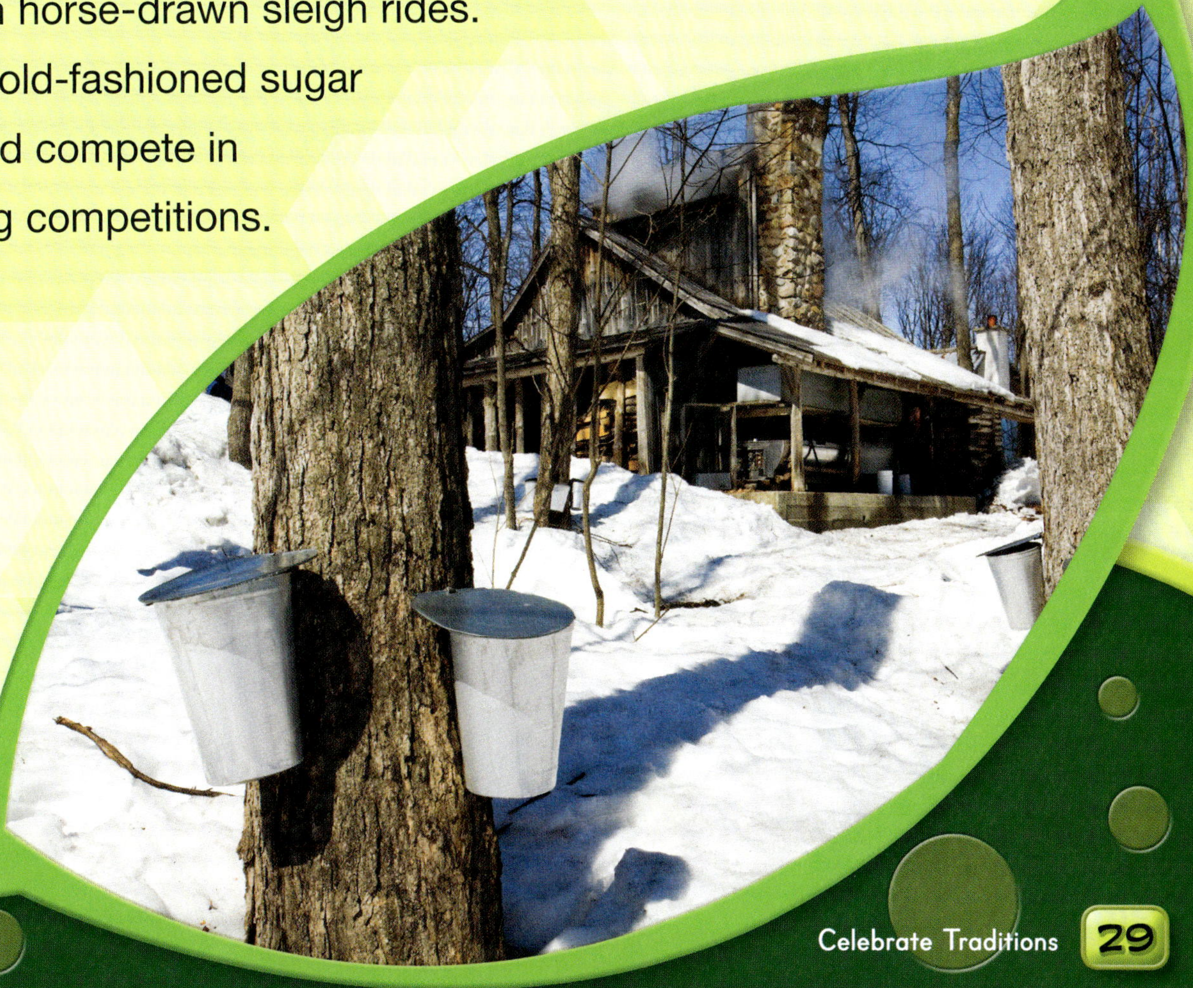

SUMMER STAMPEDE

The biggest rodeo in the world is in Calgary, Alberta, in July. Cowgirls and cowboys show off their skills in taming wild horses and fierce bulls. At the Calgary Stampede, you can see chuckwagon races, steer riding, and barrel racing. Yee haw! If you go early enough, you can even enjoy a big rodeo breakfast of pancakes and sausage.

AUTUMN WILD RICE HARVEST

Many First Nations children in Manitoba, Saskatchewan, and Ontario get to take time off school to help gather the wild rice. They use ricing sticks or knockers to knock the grains off the wild rice plants. After all the rice has been gathered, people enjoy a huge feast.

THINK ABOUT IT

What did you use to predict what this text was about?

TRY IT OUT

Predict

FUN WITH FRIENDS

by Sandy MacPherson

School today was SO MUCH FUN! It was Multicultural Day! Some kids dressed up in costumes from their culture and brought something to show.

Presents from Japan

I wore the kimono that Grandma sent me from Japan. I said the kimono was a traditional costume. Today kimonos are mostly for special events.

I also brought an origami crane that I folded myself. The crane is a symbol of peace.

Cool Stuff from Mexico

Miguel moved here from Mexico last month. He can speak Spanish and he taught me how to say a few words.

Miguel brought the coolest thing—a piñata. It was made of papier-mâché, and it was stuffed with candies. Mrs. Jordan hung it up, and we took turns hitting it with a stick to break it open. Next birthday, I'm going to ask for a piñata.

Gifts from Ukraine

Julia wore a dance costume from Ukraine. She goes to Ukrainian dance classes on Saturdays. She showed us how to do one dance. It was hard! Then we got to look at some beautiful painted eggs called pysanky. The decorations on the eggs mean different things, like good luck or good health.

Music from Scotland

Jamie brought the best thing—bagpipes! He's from Scotland and wore a kilt. He played the bagpipes and they were so loud we had to hold our hands over our ears. Jamie said that's the point—bagpipes were played in battles. They could be heard above the noise.

I'm going to ask if we can phone my grandma tonight. I want to tell her all about the fun we had today.

THINK ABOUT IT

What did you predict each section of the text was about? Were you right?

You're Invited!

Invitations ask you to come to a special event. They tell you everything you need to know about the event.

The text on an invitation tells you what the event is. It also tells you when and where it will be.

The pictures tell you more about the event. What do the pictures tell you about this event?

What does this invitation tell you?

Stay on Topic

When you pack your backpack for school, you take only those things you need for the day. You don't pack your pyjamas!

Writing is like packing your backpack. You include only those ideas you need to stay on topic.

Fall Colours **by Avery**

Every fall, my family drives up north to see the leaves change colour. I see cows on the side of the road. The leaves are red, yellow, and orange. We always stop at the same park so I can collect leaves. I eat a sandwich in the car.

In the piece of writing above, which ideas are not connected to the topic?

What do you notice about this piece of writing?

My Summer Trip **by Max**

My family goes to Scotland every summer to see my grandma. We take a plane to get there. Grandma picks us up at the airport. She always has a tin of shortbread cookies with her. Yum! We spend two weeks at her house. My favourite part of the trip is when Grandma takes us to see the old castles. Going to Scotland is a fun trip. I love seeing my grandma!

TRY IT OUT

Read Like a Writer

Standing Proud

by Roderick DiPaolo

Mr. Price's Grade 2 class had a special guest today. His name is William. He gave a speech on National Aboriginal Day. Mr. Price put William's speech and photos up on the bulletin board.

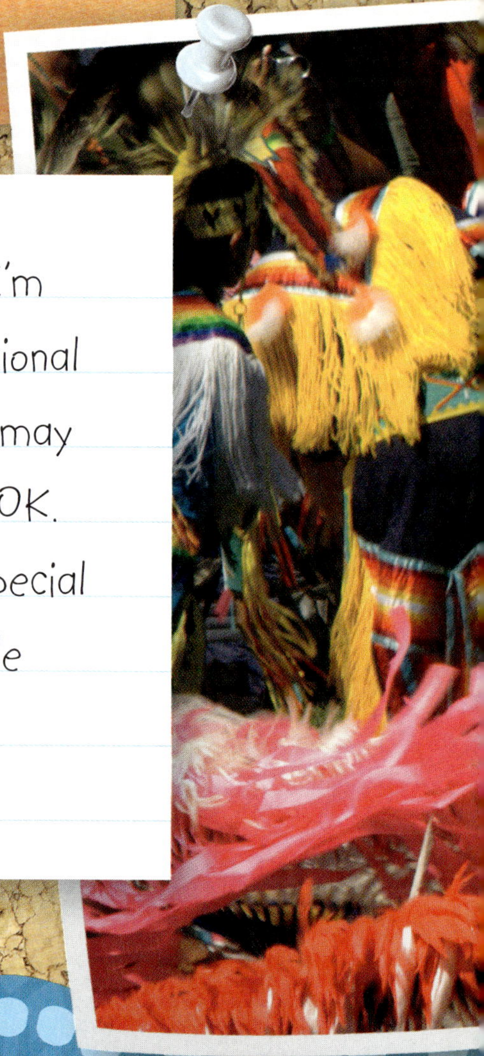

1

Hi, everyone. My name is William. I'm in Grade 4. Today I will talk about National Aboriginal Solidarity Day. Some of you may not have heard of it before, but that's OK. I'm here to tell you all about it! This special day is on June 21. This is the day people come together to celebrate Aboriginal cultures and traditions.

2 National Aboriginal Day is celebrated all across Canada. You don't have to be Aboriginal to celebrate. Everyone can listen to drummers, watch dancers, and hear an Elder tell a cool story. Last year, I danced in my first powwow. It was fun! You can also see lots of arts and crafts made by Aboriginal people.

3 Dream catchers are one example of a craft. I have one that hangs in my bedroom window. There are many things to see and do on National Aboriginal Day. People play lacrosse and have canoe races. There's a lot of delicious food, too. I think everyone should celebrate National Aboriginal Day on June 21. You will learn a lot and have a good time!

THINK ABOUT IT

Did the writer of this speech stay on topic? Can you find places in the text where he went off topic?

Credits

This page constitutes an extension of the copyright page. We have made every effort to trace the ownership of all copyrighted material and to secure permission from copyright holders. In the event of any question arising as to the use of any material, we will be pleased to make the necessary corrections in future printings. Thanks are due to the following authors, publishers, and agents for permission to use the material indicated.

Text

1-4: Illustrations © 2006 from Clara and the Bossy, written and illustrated by Ruth Ohi, published by Annick Press. Used with permission. **1-9–1-11:** Pancake Surprise by Julie Stall. **1-12–1-15:** From Hamster Chase: Based on the characters created by Ezra Jack Keats, by Anastasia Suen, illustrated by Allan Eitzen, copyright © 2001 by Ezra Jack Keats Foundation. Used by permission of Viking Children's Books, A Division of Penguin Young Readers Group, A Member of Penguin Group (USA) Inc., 345 Hudson Street, New York, NY 10014. All rights reserved. **1-16–1-19:** From The Wild, Woolly Child, text copyright © 1988 by Joy Cowley; illustrations copyright © 1988 by Philip Webb. Used with permission by Richards Literary Agency. **1-24:** Material from Stanley's Beauty Contest, written by Linda Bailey and illustrated by Bill Slavin is used by permission of Kids Can Press Ltd., Toronto. Text © 2009 Linda Bailey . Illustrations © 2009 Bill Slavin. **1-25:** Material from Suki's Kimono, written by Chieri Uegaki and illustrated by Stéphane Jorisch is used by permission of Kids Can Press Ltd., Toronto. Text © 2003 Chieri Uegaki. Illustrations ©2003 Stéphane Jorisch. **1-26–1-29:** It's Not My Fault, by Nancy Carlson. Copyright © 2003 by Nancy Carlson. Reprinted with the permission of Carolrhoda Books, a division of Lerner Publishing Group, Inc. All rights reserved. No part of this excerpt may be used or reproduced in any manner whatsoever without the prior written permission of Lerner Publishing Group, Inc. **1-30–1-32:** The Blink-Off is reproduced by permission of the publishers Learning Media Limited, PO Box 3293, Wellington, New Zealand. Text copyright © 2004 Sharon L. Norris, illustrations copyright © 2004 Ali Teo. **1-33–1-36:** Excerpt from Oonga Boonga, text copyright © 1990, 1998 by Frieda Wishinsky, illustrations © 1998 by Carol Thompson. All rights reserved. Text reproduced by permission of Scholastic Canada Ltd. Illustrations reproduced by permission of The Random House Group Ltd. Text and illustrations reproduced by permission of Dutton Children's Books, A Division of Penguin Young Readers Group, A Member of Penguin Group (USA) Inc., 345 Hudson Street, New York, NY 10014. **1-37–1-42:** From I Wanna Iguana, by Karen Kaufman Orloff, illustrated by David Catrow, copyright © 2004 by Karen Kaufman Orloff, text. Used by permission of G.P. Putnam's Sons, A Division of Penguin Young Readers Group, A Member of Penguin Group (USA) Inc., 345 Hudson Street, New York, NY 10014. All rights reserved. **2-5–2-8:** From Big Beasts, by Katherine Kenah ©2007. Used with permission by School Specialty Publishing. **2-9–2-12:** From Odd Birds, by Teresa Domnauer © 2007. Used with permission by School Specialty Publishing. **2-13–2-14:** "Jump or Jiggle" by Evelyn Beyer, from ANOTHER HERE AND NOW STORY BOOK by Lucy Sprague Mitchell, copyright 1937 by E.P. Dutton, renewed © 1965 by Lucy Sprague Mitchell. Used by permission of Dutton Children's Books, A Division of Penguin Young Readers Group, A Member of Penguin Group (USA) Inc., 345 Hudson Street, New York, NY 10014. All rights reserved. **2-15–2-18:** From Canadian Arctic Animals, by Chelsea Donaldson © 2005 by Scholastic Canada Ltd. **2-23–2-25:** Material from Owls written by Adrienne Mason, illustrated by Nancy Gray Ogle, is used by permission of Kids Can Press Ltd., Toronto. Text © 2004 Adrienne Mason. **2-34–2-35:** Mice, © 1932 by Rose Fyleman. Used with permission by The Society of Authors as the Literary Representative of the Estate of Rose Fyleman.

Photos

Cover: (giraffe) ZSSD/Minden Pictures/First Light; (inset, left) © Christopher Bernard/iStockphoto; Gelpi/shutterstock; KOUNADEAS IOANNHS/Shutterstock; Linda Webb/Shutterstock; (inset , right) © David P. Smith /Shutterstock. **1-1:** Sean Justice/Digital Vision/Getty Images. **1-2:** Russ Allen/Shutterstock. **1-3:** iStockphoto/David Olah **2-1:** (clockwise) Jerry Sharp/Shutterstock; Arnold John Labrentz/Shutterstock; fivespots/Shutterstock; Bruce MacQueen/Shutterstock. **2-2-2-3:** (background) nexus7/Shutterstock. **2-2:** (clockwise) © 2009 Jupiterimages Corporation; © 2009 Jupiterimages Corporation; Stefan Petru Andronache/Shutterstock; Thomas Mounsey/Shutterstock. **2-3:** (clockwise) Alle/Shutterstock; Eric Isselée/Shutterstock; iStockphoto/Susan Flashman; Alex James Bramwell/Shutterstock. **2-5:** (left) alphacell/Shutterstock; (inset) iStockphoto/Stefan Klein; (right) Victoria Alexandrova/Shutterstock. **2-6:** (top) iStockphoto/Jeryl Tan; (bottom) Ashley Whitworth/Shutterstock; (background) Gloria Ghiara/Shutterstock. **2-7:** (top) Dennis Donohue/Shutterstock; (bottom) Eric Isselée/Shutterstock. **2-8:** (top)

© 2009 Jupiterimages Corporation; (bottom) David B Fleetham/Oxford Scientific/Jupiter Images. **2-9–2-12:** (background) Çokeker/Shutterstock. **2-9:** Mayskyphoto/Shutterstock. **2-10:** Kristian Sekulic/Shutterstock. **2-11:** Michael Woodruff/Shutterstock. **2-12:** D McKenzie/Shutterstock. **2-13:** (top) Anna Diederich /Shutterstock; (bottom) iStockphoto/Arturo Limon. **2-14:** (top) Drazen Vukelic/Shutterstock; (bottom) © 2009 Jupiterimages Corporation. **2-15:** Daniel Cox /Oxford Scientific/Jupiter Images. **2-16:** (top) © 2009 Jupiterimages Corporation; (bottom) Natalia Bratslavsky/Shutterstock. **2-17:** Thorsten Milse/Robert Harding/Jupiter Images. **2-18:** Chad Ehlers/Stock Connection/Jupiter Images. **2-19–2-22:** (background) Carsten Reisinger/Shutterstock. **2-19:** (top) Michael Klenetsky/Shutterstock; (bottom) Gary Meszaros/Visuals Unlimited/Getty Images. **2-21:** (top) Sebastian Duda/Shutterstock; (right) Michael Steden/Shutterstock. **2-22:** (top) Minden Pictures/First Light; (right) Minden Pictures/First Light. **2-23–2-25:** (backgrounds) artcalin/Shutterstock; sabri deniz kizil/Shutterstock. **2-23:** (clockwise) iStockphoto/Anna Yu; Awe Inspiring Images/Shutterstock; Eric Gevaert/Shutterstock. **2-24:** iStockphoto/Jill Lang. **2-24–2-25:** Minden Pictures/First Light. **2-26–2-29:** (background) Tatiana53/Shutterstock. **2-26:** A.G.E. Fotostock/First Light. **2-27:** iStockphoto/John Anderson. **2-28:** (top) © Mb-fotos/Dreamstime; (bottom) Norbert Rosing/National Geographic/Getty Images. **2-29:** (top) Photo Researchers/First Light; (bottom) © 2009 Jupiterimages Corporation. **2-30:** Robert Sarosiek/Shutterstock; **2-31**: (top) David B Fleetham/Oxford Scientific/Jupiter Images; (bottom) © F. Lukasseck/Masterfile. **2-32:** (top) Laurie Excell/Fogstock/A.G.E. Fotostock; (middle) kwest/Shutterstock. **2-33:** (top) Michael Redmer/Visuals Unlimited/Getty Images; (bottom) IntraClique LLC/Shutterstock. **2-34:** Edyta Pawlowska/Shutterstock. **2-36:** Vladimir Chernyanskiy/Shutterstock. **2-37:** Brian L. Lambert/Shutterstock. **2-40–2-42:** (background) © iStockphoto/Russell Tate . **2-40:** (middle) © Wolfgang Kaehler/CORBIS; (bottom) iStockphoto/Paul Loewen. **2-41:** (clockwise) Photo © Canadian Museum of Civilization, artifact IV-C-3232, image D2004-01723; Sam Chadwick/Shutterstock; A.G.E. Fotostock/First Light. **2-42:** (top) Photo © Canadian Museum of Civilization, artifact IV-C-4461 a-b, image D2005-12331; (bottom) Photo © Canadian Museum of Civilization, artifact IV-B-1682, image D2005-21227. **3-1:** © Serega/Dreamstime. **3-2:** (Clockwise) The Canadian Press (London Free Press-Morris Lamont); Tobin Grimshaw/Toronto Star; Bushnell/Soifer/Stone/Getty Images. **3-3:** (Clockwise) © CLARENCE W. NORRIS ALL RIGHTS RESERVED; Rodolfo Arpia/Alamy; Roger Charity/Stock Image/Jupiter Images. **3-4:** (clockwise) © Serega/Dreamstime; © photolibrary. All rights reserved; Joe Pitz/Shutterstock; © Craig Aurness/CORBIS; © WAYNE SHIELS ALL RIGHTS RESERVED; Rodolfo Arpia/Alamy. **3-5:** Ron Bull/Toronto Star. **3-6:** (top) Rene Johnston/Toronto Star; (bottom) © WAYNE SHIELS ALL RIGHTS RESERVED. **3-7:** (top) The Canadian Press (Charlottetown Guardian - Brian McInnis); (bottom) The Canadian Press (Jonathan Hayward). **3-12:** © CLARENCE W. NORRIS ALL RIGHTS RESERVED. **3-13:** (top) The Canadian Press (Edmonton Sun-Darryl Dyck); (bottom) Andersen Ross/Stockbyte/Getty Images. **3-14:** (left and right) Photos by Lois Siegel. **3-15:** (top) © 2009 Jupiterimages Corporation; (bottom) Elena Elisseeva/Shutterstock. **3-16:** (top inset clockwise) Kevin Wheal/Alamy; Freddy Eliasson/Shutterstock; Elena Moiseeva/Shutterstock; Kirill Kurashov/Shutterstock; (bottom) Simon Reddy/Alamy. **3-17:** © Pureradian/Dreamstime. **3-1–3-19:** (background) karanta/Shutterstock. **3-18:** Steve Cukrov/Shutterstock. **3-19:** (clockwise) Robyn Mackenzie/Shutterstock; Dariusz Sas/Shutterstock; Jill Battaglia/Shutterstock; Madeleine Openshaw/Shutterstock. **3-20–3-23:** (background) Roman Sigaev/Shutterstock. **3-20:** View Stock/Alamy. **3-21:** Nathan Benn/Alamy. **3-22:** © Ajay Verma/Reuters/Corbis. **3-23:** (top) Howard Sandler/Shutterstock; (bottom) Photo by John McCusker © 2009 The Times-Picayune Publishing Co., all rights reserved. Used with permission of The Times-Picayune. **3-24:** (background) © iStockphoto/Melanie Taylor; Patrick Olear/PhotoEdit Inc. **3-25:** (top) © Batman2000/Dreamstime; (bottom) © Kwame Zikomo/SuperStock. **3-26:** © Bennym/Dreamstime. **3-27:** Kayte M. Deioma/PhotoEdit Inc. **3-28:** © photolibrary. All rights reserved. **3-29:** (top) Megapress/Alamy; (bottom) Yves Marcoux/First Light. **3-30:** (top) Larry MacDougal/First Light; (bottom) The Canadian Press (Jeff McIntosh). **3-31:** (top) The Canadian Press (AP Photo/Jim Mone); (bottom) Mona Makela/Shutterstock. **3-32–3-35:** (backgrounds) Max Bukovski/Shutterstock; Attsetski/Shutterstock. **3-32:** (middle) Armand Harris/Alamy; (bottom) ultimathule/Shutterstock. **3-33:** (top) Dan Bigelow/The Image Bank/Getty Images; (bottom) Jeffrey Coolidge/Stone/Getty Images. **3-34:** (top left) © Craig Aurness/CORBIS; (right) © iStockphoto/Dmitriy Tereschenko. **3-35:** Leland Bobbe/Photodisc/Getty Images. **3-36:** (clockwise) Jose Gil/Shutterstock; Philip Scalia/Alamy; Cynthia Farmer/Shutterstock; Duncan Davis/Alamy. **3-40:** (background) Michael Levy/Shutterstock. **3-40–3-42:** (background) dakolix/Shutterstock. **3-40–3-41:** Emily Riddell/First Light. **3-42:** © Nikitu/Dreamstime.

Art

All robots by Dan Hambe. **1-2–3:** James Yamasaki. **1-22–23:** Brian McLachlan. **2-4:** Anton Petrov. **2-20:** Ann Sanderson. **2-34–35:** Sally Wern Comport. **2-38–39:** Brian McLachlan. **3-6–7:** Deborah Crowle. **3-17:** Deborah Crowle. **3-37:** Jan John Rivera. **3-38–39:** Brian McLachlan.